OUR SOLAR SYSTEM

SATURN

Susan Ring

AV² provides enriched content that supplements and complements this book. Weigl's AV² books strive to create inspired learning and engage young minds in a total learning experience.

Your AV² Media Enhanced books come alive with...

Audio
Listen to sections of the book read aloud.

Key Words
Study vocabulary, and complete a matching word activity.

Video
Watch informative video clips.

Quizzes
Test your knowledge.

Go to **www.av2books.com**, and enter this book's unique code.

Embedded Weblinks
Gain additional information for research.

Slide Show
View images and captions, and prepare a presentation.

BOOK CODE

Q607107

AV² **by Weigl** brings you media enhanced books that support active learning.

Try This!
Complete activities and hands-on experiments.

... and much, much more!

Published by AV² by Weigl
350 5th Avenue, 59th Floor
New York, NY 10118
Website: www.av2books.com   www.weigl.com

Library of Congress Cataloging-in-Publication Data

Ring, Susan.
Saturn / Susan Ring.
    p. cm. -- (Our solar system)
Audience: 4-6.
Includes index.
ISBN 978-1-62127-268-7 (hardcover : alk. paper) -- ISBN 978-1-62127-277-9 (softcover : alk. paper)
1. Saturn (Planet)--Juvenile literature. I. Title. II. Series: Our solar system (AV2 by Weigl)
QB671.R56 2014
523.46--dc23

                      2012044380

Printed in the United States of America in Brainerd, Minnesota
2 3 4 5 6 7 8 9 0 19 18 17 16 15

102015
131015

Project Coordinator Aaron Carr
Editorial BLPS Content Connections
Designer Mandy Christiansen

Every reasonable effort has been made to trace ownership and to obtain permission to reprint copyright material. The publishers would be pleased to have any errors or omissions brought to their attention so that they may be corrected in subsequent printings.

Photo Credits
Weigl acknowledges Getty Images as as its primary photo supplier for this title. Other sources: NASA: page 7 (Saturn & Moons), NASA: page 11 (Saturn).

Contents

Introducing Saturn

There are three types of planets in the **solar system**: rocky planets, **Gas Giants**, and **Ice Giants**. The planet Saturn is one of the two Gas Giants. Saturn is best known for its rings. People discover new information about this planet almost daily. Read on to learn more about the second-largest planet in the solar system.

Until 1977, scientists believed Saturn was the only planet with rings.

Saturn Facts

- The rings around Saturn are not solid. They are made of billions of pieces of rock and ice. Some of these are tiny pieces of dust. Others are mountain-sized boulders.

- Saturn is not the only planet with rings. Jupiter, Uranus, and Neptune also have rings. Saturn's rings are the easiest to see.

- Saturn's rings span up to 175,000 miles (282,000 kilometers). The rings are 0.6 miles (1 km) thick.

- Earth is about 10 times closer to the Sun than Saturn.

- Saturn is slightly smaller in size than Jupiter, but Jupiter is more than three times heavier.

Naming the Planet

Saturn is the ancient Roman god of farming. Saturn is also a god of time. This might be why the planet Saturn is named after him. Of all the planets known in ancient Roman times, Saturn had the slowest **orbit** around the Sun. In Greek **mythology**, Saturn is known as Cronus. He is the son of Uranus.

The word "Saturday" comes from the word "Saturn." Ancient Romans called the seventh day of the week *Dies Saturni*, which means "Saturn's Day."

Cronus was made to hold the world on his back as punishment after his son took control of the gods.

Saturn's Moons

People once thought that Saturn had 18 moons. Now, scientists recognize 53 moons around Saturn. There may be even more moons that have not yet been discovered.

Saturn's largest moon is called Titan. It is the only moon in Earth's solar system known to have an **atmosphere**.

The moons Pandora and Prometheus are called shepherd moons. This is because their **gravity** holds one of Saturn's rings in place.

Together, Saturn and its moons are called the Saturnian System.

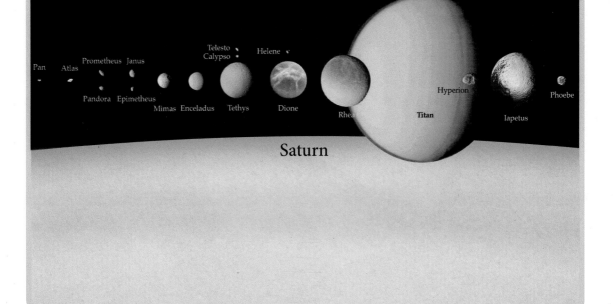

First Sightings

Saturn was first seen through a telescope in 1610. An Italian **astronomer** named Galileo Galilei saw it. He did not know there were rings around Saturn. Instead, Galileo saw the planet and its rings as three orbs. The middle orb, Saturn, appeared three times as large as the orbs on each side. Galileo thought the smaller orbs were moons. In his drawings of the planet, Saturn looks like it has ears.

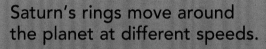
Saturn's rings move around the planet at different speeds.

Life on Saturn?

Saturn is mostly made of hydrogen and helium. Saturn is also very cold and has fast winds. It is unlikely anything could live on Saturn.

Some scientists believe that Saturn's moon Titan could support life. The temperature on Titan is very cold, but Titan does have an atmosphere. Like Earth, the atmosphere is mostly made up of nitrogen. Scientists also believe there is water beneath the surface of Titan.

Titan is the second-largest known moon in the solar system.

Spotting Saturn

Sky watchers could see Saturn long before telescopes were invented. Saturn was one of five planets known to ancient people. From Earth, Saturn looks like a bright, yellowish star.

Saturn is tilted as it spins on its **axis**. Because of this, there are times when the planet's rings are hard to see. Saturn's rings appear to vanish twice during its orbit around the Sun. The rings can only be seen through a telescope.

Saturn's farthest ring is also its biggest. Its height is about 20 times the width of the planet.

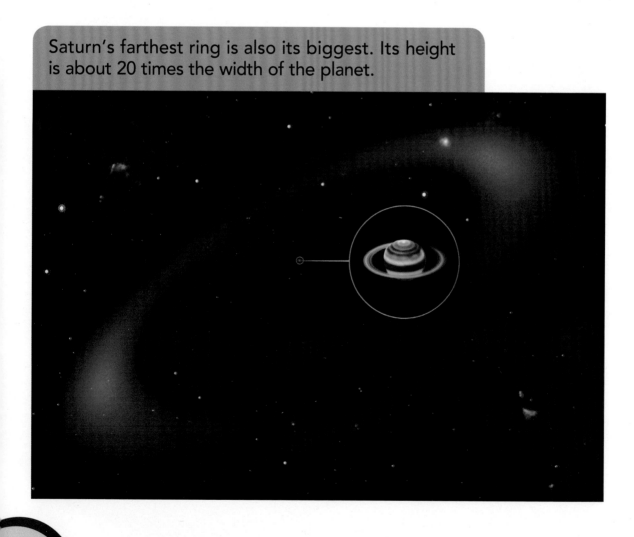

See for Yourself

When you see Saturn in the sky, it looks like a star. How can you tell if you are looking at a planet or a star? They both shine brightly, but planets do not shimmer and twinkle. Planets shine with a steady light. Saturn shines more brightly in April, when it is closest to Earth.

When viewed through a telescope, Saturn appears to have yellow bands. These are caused by Saturn's fast winds and heat rising from inside the planet.

Charting Our Solar System

Earth's solar system is made up of eight planets, five known dwarf planets, and many other space objects, such as **asteroids** and **comets**. Saturn is the sixth planet from the Sun.

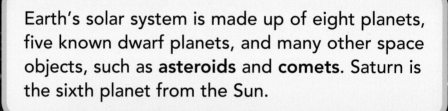

Sun

Venus

Mercury

Earth

Mars

Ceres

Jupiter

Order of Planets

Here is an easy way to remember the order of the planets from the Sun. Take the first letter of each planet, from Mercury to Neptune, and make it into a sentence. <u>M</u>y <u>V</u>ery <u>E</u>nthusiastic <u>M</u>other <u>J</u>ust <u>S</u>erved <u>U</u>s <u>N</u>oodles.

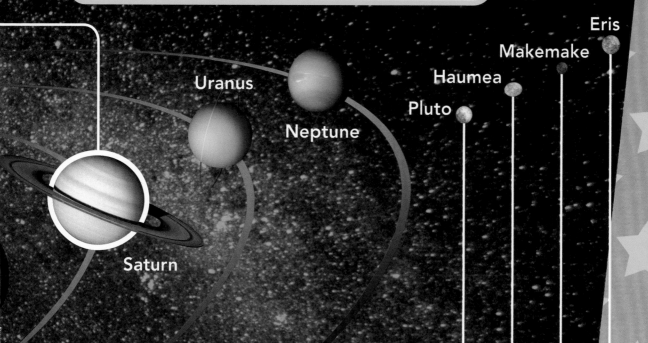

Eris

Makemake

Uranus

Haumea

Neptune

Pluto

Saturn

Dwarf Planets

A dwarf planet is a round object that orbits the Sun. It is larger than an asteroid or comet but smaller than a planet.

Moons are not dwarf planets because they do not orbit the Sun directly. They orbit other planets.

Saturn and Earth

Saturn does not have a solid surface, like Earth. However, it has almost the exact same gravity as Earth. In other words, a person would weigh the same on Saturn as on Earth.

A year on Saturn lasts 30 years on Earth. Saturn rotates on its axis once every 10 hours and 32 minutes. It takes Earth 24 hours to rotate once on its axis.

Saturn is about nine times bigger around than Earth.

**Earth's diameter
7,926 miles
(12,756 km)**

**Saturn's diameter
74,975 miles
(120,650 km)**

Comparing the Planets

Planets (by distance from the Sun)	Distance from the Sun	Days to orbit the Sun	Diameter	Length of Day	Mean Temperature
Mercury	36 million miles (58 million km)	88 Earth Days	3,032 miles (4,880 km)	1,408 hours	354°F (179°C)
Venus	67 million miles (108 million km)	225 Earth Days	7,521 miles (12,104 km)	5,832 hours	847°F (453°C)
Earth	93 million miles (150 million km)	365 Earth Days	7,926 miles (12,756 km)	24 hours	46°F (8°C)
Mars	142 million miles (228 million km)	687 Earth Days	4,217 miles (6,787 km)	24.6 hours	−82°F (−63°C)
Jupiter	484 million miles (778 million km)	4,333 Earth Days	88,732 miles (142,800 km)	10 hours	−244°F (−153°C)
Saturn	887 million miles (1,427 million km)	10,756 Earth Days	74,975 miles (120,660 km)	11 hours	−301°F (−185°C)
Uranus	1,784 million miles (2,871 million km)	30,687 Earth Days	31,763 miles (51,118 km)	17 hours	−353°F (−214°C)
Neptune	2,795 million miles (4,498 million km)	60,190 Earth Days	30,775 miles (49,528 km)	16 hours	−373°F (−225°C)

Saturn Today

Astronomers are learning new things about Saturn almost every day. This is because a spacecraft is orbiting Saturn right now. That spacecraft is called *Cassini*.

NASA launched *Cassini* in 1997. The *Cassini* orbiter carried a European **space probe** called *Huygens* to Saturn. It took seven years to get there. *Cassini* will continue to orbit Saturn until 2017.

The *Huygens* space probe was sent to gather information about Saturn's rings and moons. The probe landed on the surface of Saturn's largest moon, Titan.

Voyager 2
Launch 1977
Vehicle Flyby

Huygens
Launch 2004
Vehicle Lander

Voyager 1
Launch 1977
Vehicle Flyby

Pioneer 11
Launch 1973
Vehicle Flyby

Cassini
Launch 2004
Vehicle Orbiter

17

Planet Watchers

Christiaan Huygens discovered Saturn's rings

About 50 years after Galileo wrote about Saturn, a Dutch astronomer named Christiaan Huygens made another discovery. He realized that the bulges on either side of Saturn were rings. Huygens also discovered Titan, Saturn's biggest moon.

Christiaan Huygens found a new method of grinding and polishing lenses. The improved lenses helped him to discover Saturn's rings.

Carolyn C. Porco heads the Cassini-Huygens team

Carolyn C. Porco is an expert on rings around planets. She studies the rings around Neptune and Uranus. Porco is in charge of the team that collects and stores photographs taken by the *Cassini-Huygens* probe.

Porco's ideas about space have been used in movies and television. She has contributed a great deal to space exploration. In fact, an asteroid was named Porco in her honor.

Carolyn Porco worked on the team that studied data from Uranus and Neptune. The data was collected during the *Voyager* missions.

What Have You Learned?

Take this quiz to test your knowledge of Saturn.

1 Saturn is the closest planet to the Sun. True or False?

2 What are Saturn's rings made of?

3 What is the name of Saturn's largest moon?

4 How long does a year on Saturn last?

5 What is the name of the spacecraft orbiting Saturn right now?

6 What did Galileo Galilei think Saturn's rings were when he first saw them?

7 Why are some moons called shepherd moons?

8 Which day of the week is named for Saturn?

9 What is the name of the space probe that visited Titan?

10 What do the atmospheres of Titan and Earth have in common?

Young Scientists at Work

Ring Art

Saturn's rings are made up of many chunks of ice and rock. From far away, the rings look like solid bands. Why is this?

You will need:

- a blank sheet of paper
- a black marker

1. Use a marker to make a circle using 40 to 50 tiny dots (rather than a solid line).

2. Tape the paper to a wall. Notice how you can see the separate dots when you are standing close to the paper.

3. Slowly back up while looking at the paper. Do you notice that the dots appear to join together? From far away, they look like a solid line in the shape of a circle.

Saturn's rings are thought to be pieces of comets, asteroids, and moons. They broke up into smaller pieces before entering Saturn's atmosphere.

Key Words

asteroids: small, solid objects in space that circle the Sun

astronomer: person who studies space and its objects

atmosphere: the layer of gases surrounding a planet

axis: an imaginary line on which a planet spins

comets: small objects in space made from dust and ice

Gas Giants: large planets in Earth's solar system made mostly of gas. Jupiter and Saturn are the two Gas Giants in our solar system.

gravity: a force that pulls things toward the center

Ice Giants: very cold giant planets. Neptune and Uranus are the two Ice Giants in the solar system.

mythology: stories or legends, often about gods or heroes

NASA: National Aeronautics and Space Administration; part of U.S. government responsible for space research

orbit: the nearly circular path a space object makes around another object in space

solar system: the Sun, the planets, and other objects that move around the Sun

space probe: spacecraft used to gather information about space

Index

Log on to www.av2books.com

AV² by Weigl brings you media enhanced books that support active learning. Go to www.av2books.com, and enter the special code found on page 2 of this book. You will gain access to enriched and enhanced content that supplements and complements this book. Content includes video, audio, weblinks, quizzes, a slide show, and activities.

AV² Online Navigation

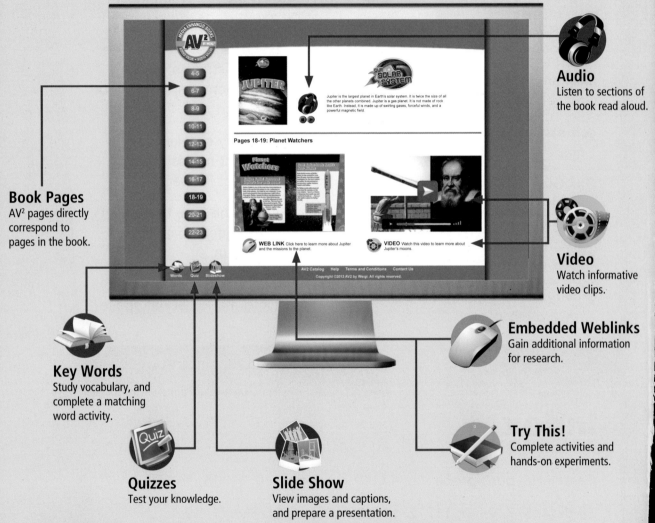

Audio
Listen to sections of the book read aloud.

Book Pages
AV² pages directly correspond to pages in the book.

Video
Watch informative video clips.

Key Words
Study vocabulary, and complete a matching word activity.

Embedded Weblinks
Gain additional information for research.

Try This!
Complete activities and hands-on experiments.

Quizzes
Test your knowledge.

Slide Show
View images and captions, and prepare a presentation.

AV² was built to bridge the gap between print and digital. We encourage you to tell us what you like and what you want to see in the future.

Sign up to be an AV² Ambassador at www.av2books.com/ambassador.